ozark love poems & a song of divinity

nettie zan powers

Spartan Press

Spartan Press
Kansas City, Missouri
spartanpresskc.com

Copyright © Nettie Zan Powers, 2021
First Edition: 1 3 5 7 9 10 8 6 4 2
ISBN: 978-1-952411-89-2
LCCN: 2021951337

Cover photo: Nettie Zan
Author photo: Nettie Zan
All rights reserved. No part of this publication may be reproduced or transmitted in any form or by any means, electronic or mechanical, including photocopying, recording or by info retrieval system, without prior written permission from the author.

note from the poet:

the 20 love sonnets within
are lightly riffing on pablo neruda's
legendary book of 100 love sonnets
the title of the book pays homage
to his book "20 love poems
and a song of despair."

to the ozarks
which holds space for this holy fool

ozark love poems

i

ozarks: the name of a ridge, an orchid, a watershed
of things that hover over the earth and ascend
a word where opening bliss first arises
in whose winter the spring water thirsts

ozark glades and cedars grow through that name
and the clear-earnest creeks surround them
its letters are the shore of otter's play
that brighten my haunted heart

oh name that rests undisturbed in cat briar
like an aperture to a secret voluminous cave
kissing the karst of the deep plateau's uplift

explore me with the gloss of your jewel weed; investigate me
with your green snake eyes -- if you like -- only allow me
to hold this place in my mouth and open my voice for you

ii

stinging nettle, a lavender with its thistle
of bite and thorn of thriving honey locust
arrow of time, impertinence: i surrender this life to you
what piercing greening brought you?

why did you set wildfire, living spark
sudden rampant over my sturdy bluff?
who told you how to find me? what wild parsnip
what dolomite, what fog lead you to undertake me?

because of you -- the river which flows beneath does rise
the fog caresses each opening into the cavernous dark
and arises in cool mist to comfort thirsty ghosts

when you shed a tear, it falls from my eye
this relentless love -- even your fenced heart, your echoes
brand my divinity with the richness of black walnut blossoms

iii

you will remember lapping the pooling spring
where cracked mud receded and broke
and here a cairn, unsteady mound of rocks
covering the dust of your birth

you will remember the grief of the earth
puppy breath, a smoke ring flittering away
tea of rose hips and the losses of native arrows
ten centuries away from this stack of boulders

you'll remember the ledge
beneath the cliff against the creek
shadows and silent water

that time was like never, and like always
we are here, where nothing waits
and sitting here in a place with nowhere to go

iv

i do not hold your river or your creek or the white crests
only the length of the rocky bed, the bend, confluence
persimmons bruised on the forest floor
the shoal and chute which cannot be resisted

from the north fork of the whites of your eyes
to the broad ridge in the south, the post oak to the pines
you are the red clay of deep missouri, pressing my thumbs
into the heft of your curves, i hold spring itself

you are all potential and i love your chance as a dream i hid
from my lonesome self, i shaped mountains into your likeness
before the portent of knowing what you are like

and then, when you are there with me
you are the light i allow to leave me exposed
i shudder in ecstasy and surrender to your dominion

V

here i am, i said, although i know
what echo of distilled pain i hold
now boots have crushed the flower of me
a footprint on my offered neck

i say it again, *here i am*, i have already died
the moon has drowned me silent, the sun blinded me
vast rampage of society's howling madness
and my love, i only offer to forget it all!

i gift you a purity, that you might never
pay for a debt of scars you do not owe
that only i, *here i am*, stand innocent now

in this grace, there is a tiny chasm
which may hold every tempest, all the storms of you
blood and blade, the hidden violence, and the hidden joy

vi

if your body were not scarred by weight, canyons of damage
and labor and if even your broken heart were no cage
but the flushed wingbeat of a nighthawk at dusk on the current
if you were not the orange good-bye kiss of sunset

not the violet sky behind a black silhouette
when saturn overcomes the wandering giant
if you were not the simmering broth
of distilled bones and fat

oh, storm of wild flowers, then i could only love you half-way
but when i hold you, i want the stretch, the watermark, the scar
the all-the-ways of your torn land stitching itself once more

everything made us breathless
and yet we live, the horror and the awe
your wide and stout thighs holding both of us

vii

there where the maul cleaves the fallen ash
a cracking division, irreparable form
the inner circle of rings falling into isolated arcs
always the sharp of the passing blade

oh bright axe, surrender to the gravity
aim for the center of the dancing earth
and orbit -- movement, still -- infinite
carved wood, fractal rounds of the spinning forest

shoulder and chest, the cartwheeling bicep and hand
light motion within motion, nested cycles, cured and uncured
the ten thousand centers wheeling and integral and dividing

this swing through heart wood, falling timber
persistent grain, knuckle, acorn plunging
we make the only possible choice

viii

this beauty is winsome, as if song and thunder
lace and glass, bonfire and candle
that gutters and gasps in the wind
has made me into a fleeting statue

toes in cold spring water, wrapped
in watercress and nibbled by minnows
ankles maypoling to hips, the confluence
of a prayer at my chest, the stone beneath

beatific, between being, i will not be set against myself
supplicant, steel, i am everything that can be
stunning creature, formless form of weaving grace

at my fissures, where oppositions crumble
my performance is all ice and inferno -- a held breath
water taking shape, the air assembling storms

ix

i request nothing less than my freedom
unbounded and spontaneous, you may track my movements
put your nose to the ground and find me, hunt
for this magnetism as though it is your religion

i thirst for only spring water, so brand new
to the moonlight of my hands, bound to this array of land
cupped and offering the split persimmon of my lips
find me at branching of the little finger west of the eagle's nest

i bite the abandon of breath
the wandering compass of liberation
i am contained by this gift and never confined

when you are starving at the forest's edge
i am yearning pursuit and laughing plenty
edge closer, warm joy, eyes and lips and *yes*

X

full creature, wild honeysuckle, hidden moon
fingers of trout lily, compost and seeds
saved from the harvest, a held promise of flowers
bouqueting on the savage plains of your chest

oh love is a journey of earthworms and stars
of suffocating expanses and floods of frost
love is a strike of fireflies
two bodies melded by one honey

nose to nose i invite your little infinity
your shore, your perimeter, the house of your hearth fire
and the cup of your sex -- cocoon, ravenous --

sinking past the water's surface with empty lungs
till gasping i breathe the water of your pleasure
am catfish, am bottom feeder, am shimmer in dark springs

xi

something luminescent glows from your moon face
the dark power of underground rivers, a surfacing
spring water in your sumac eyes, it is not glinting quartz
or cold steel, you are the transmutation of tea leaves

the calendula and rose hips grow for your omens
what practiced patience steeps the medicines
you, divinity, keeping grace in the offering cup of solace
dandelion root, changeling of the perimeter

oh, leaves at the crest of your neck
your glancing shoulder, lavender broth
my love, warm throat of the morning

ozark waters, flowing uphill through rock
carving the honeycomb cauldron of the land
deep pressure, finding its way to my lips

xii

the ozarks have been calling for you to return
today, an aeon ago, her untouched caves
they did not know your name
only your body, the gravity of water, your mineral parts

there is within you, an aspect which hears the cedar ridge
an inner you keen to tree frogs and coyotes and kingfishers
the spring water of your body hums in tune
with the eleven point river and her two blue creeks

somewhere between the grips of your atoms
in the vast emptiness within all that appears solid
is a vibration singing harmony, this is the call

we who magnetize back will name this *significance*
will understand the constancy of vetch and witch hazel
breathe the cycle only as it comes, patient and wild

xiii

here with the creek at her shut-ins
where the hewn bedrock surfaces
this wound, this waterfall
this place the witch hazel blooms

despite the bleak of january
and her blinding glare on the water
colder, now, even than the springs
only those of us in need of baptism enter her now

it is called falling because there is no turning back
we haven't the luxury of being against gravity
our riches are no reprieve from the heart's plunging

snow lingers in the shade of small bluffs
i take off my shoes, one by one, deliberate
i enter the cold, rippling water toes first

xiv

my foolhardy heaven, you are the surge and the whirlpool
my reckless existence, you are the detritus of flood
terrible: you are the restless moment made present
lovely: the river zephyr which lifts all tarps downstream

horrible: your tempation is the edge of a soaring bluff
incredible: i am no longer afraid of heights
where did you learn to careen so effortlessly
with the grace of planets in retrograde

ugly: there is a dark blossom inside you
which i will meet, deaf and blind
beauty: seed by seed, i will grow a forest with you

my terror: i love you for your quaking power
my sanctuary: for the folding in of our bodies in prayer
i love you for what you tear apart and for what you build

XV

where you are lost, i become a glimmer
and breathed into your lungs
maybe it was an infinite void whispering back
a cracked bell, or medicine

something very near, an abiding secret
grief between us we must be witness to
two hands dancing in a dirge
against the pressing black flat truth of graves

awakening is a gift of my luminescence
the star-fire under my tongue, the opening throat
scintillating abandon turning the crescent moon full

as if you never were left behind
as if the ozarks of your childhood persisted
a trail of breadcrumbs, the smell of wood fire

xvi

missouri-love, the wind picked up the voice of the sycamores
like elegant water bringers in the mists over the south ridge
and it all glows in white, breaching the sky
embracing the bank, sand and churt, everything exiled together

come see the crawfish at the creek's edge
the pinching all of the universe, so quick, red and flying backwards
from shadows, come touch the bliss of this momentary green
before norfork lake floods the lowlands of the old river

here are countless greens -- nascent, eternal, fecund, viridian --
we are sometimes lost, can we bring ourselves to the altar
the power of roots, the unlocking of the ozark's divine words

there's nothing here except bright presence, arrangement
of matter, a hymnal among leaves and breezes
till the void gives up their secret of seeds

xvii

neither the summer sky or the color of blue spring
nor the cunning ridge of the devil's backbone
no cold has numbed my soul, no drought has left me desiccated
i am water-rich, replete in the creek's love affair with the bedrock

oh my wonder, i have never seen before now
this is the perseverance of winter my hands form
the high truth of cycles because of the quiet
of sun on toes and the ache of distant stars

what light of god's language dances on the water?
what resilience of cat briar in the underbrush?
everywhere there is purity, the earth has imitated you

who answers anger with curiosity, who embraces pain and says
only *look how strong we are*, who lifts the chin
of the vicious and kisses their bared teeth

xviii

love, from wound to wound, precipice to precipice
the world has been churning beneath us
our hearts either invisible or targets
still we have grown mulberries and children

everywhere we have been, the arrows
have glanced us, we are the narrow miss
where they have speared our siblings
we have cultivated strength from loss

we have learned to pray with cut tongues
we have sung at the fire while the forest burned
our tattoos and scars a gospel of what will not be forgotten

we go on gathering our queer animals to lick clean
to hold hands when the gravestones grow pillows
offering kisses when we falter before the face of god

xix

i have never spent a wish on anything except *let it be*
skin made of impenetrable translucence
a persistence of joy, living out of boxes
small anarchist of how and why and what it all means

i see the eyes of a bat in broad daylight
i have looked into the sun until
i can see my own heart's open path
into bliss from the dark

light is the bones of my skeleton
instability is my foundation
there is nothing to measure myself against

when you see my quaking edge
my crumbling heart is offering to you
come to know the face of my unborn soul

XX

mythical being of my awakening heart
with your spider web veils and osprey feet
the foam of your songbody falls downstream
into this land those with dashed hopes call *make-believe*

i hold the surrendering rapids of my crests
i hold my head high and breathe pure air
surrounded by your flood of silt and churning mud
you hold me above the river's surge

neither myself nor the water may be grasped in a fist
wisdom may only be offered and never taken
one can only have pleasure if one gives it

half creek water, half rich humus
this beating life is a being of multiple worlds
where i must leave everything behind to find myself

a song of divinity

you wounded healer
i have come to you wretched and revoked

only to find an empty fountain
and learn to live thirsty

i have tried to expire for love
i have tried to conjure no self

so i wouldn't consume love faithlessly
so i would learn to live in absence like you

you trick of no tricks
i have sacrificed the ten thousand things

and still find myself shoeless and silent
sweeping up the shrapnel of your humor

a cut lip, blood on a stubbed out cigarette
mold on shower tiles, the death mother grieving

a phone call from when I was eleven years old
with all of my ghosts on the dead line

oh abandoned maker, how you have seeded menageries
to fill your loneliness and how we hunger for you

a duststorm on the plains, the last ivory-billed woodpecker
children who have never slept under the stars

a dejected teenager committed only to their glowing hand
locking themselves in a room of plastic and artificial light

your providence is in the gift our of imaginations
we must invent mercy again and forgive ourselves finally

i seek you in my tea leaves, fingernail clippings
the fog of dawn in the ozark valley

oh great spirit, i can't tell the difference between you
and the bit of perseverence that arises me from sleep

i cast a primal spell to lose everything
because no object, no thought

no lucky number, no home, no habit
turned out to have any answers

you unrooted root
how did we get here and how

do we get out of this cluttered chaos
and what measure marks out a good life

oh holy fool, i wish only to make good
of a world overrun by hoarded stores of uselessness

a pretend value of bottled water and souvenirs
when nothing survives the final breath

can something beautiful
still be pulled from the wreckage

i hold a dead bouquet of wildflowers
and tell you it means hope

oh divinity, oh sacred fount of infinity
thy will be done and not mine

and yet we are all one
where do i end and you begin

am i praying to myself in the dark hours
of affliction and remorse, the quilted pain of grandmothers

is there solace in a line of verse or waiting for bread to rise
can we surrender from the murdering ancestors

i forgive you, you sacred heathen
for not knowing how to condemn tyranny

i forgive you for the pain of birth and for your averted gaze
upon the misery of orphans and slaves and extinctions

i forgive you as i must forgive myself
being descended from your saintly loins

you divine desecration
i accept your gift of a squandered eden

because it is your legacy
because i have my own design for tomorrow

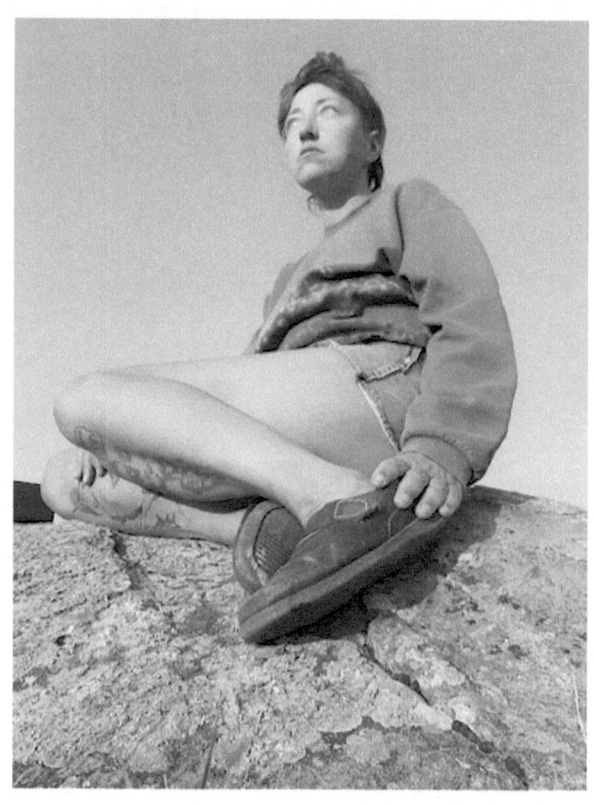

nettie zan powers is the author of several books of poetry and novels, a painter, drawer and naturalist. they are happiest on river banks communing with the wild and friends.

@listenmore

strange.gen.et@gmail.com

www.ingramcontent.com/pod-product-compliance
Lightning Source LLC
Chambersburg PA
CBHW022014120526
44592CB00034B/1003